L O G I C
L I F T O F F

Written by Bonnie Risby

Illustrated by Dean Crawford

First published in 2007 by Prufrock Press Inc.

Published in 2021 by Routledge
605 Third Avenue, New York, NY 10017
2 Park Square, Milton Park, Abingdon, Oxon OX14 4RN

Routledge is an imprint of the Taylor & Francis Group, an informa business

Copyright © 2007 by Taylor & Francis Group

ISBN: 9781593630881 (pbk)

DOI: 10.4324/9781003236269

For the Instructor

About this book

Logic Liftoff is designed to appeal to the innate curiosity of fourth, fifth, and sixth graders. It is filled with puzzles, mazes, and strategy maneuvers designed to delight the imagination and sharpen critical thinking skills. Through *Logic Liftoff*, young minds will encounter the thinking methods perfected by thinkers through the ages. The format of the book, however, is such that young thinkers are piqued by new adventures in puzzle solving.

The skills students build by using this book are applicable to several areas of the curriculum. Academic skills used in reading, math, writing, and science all depend on the ability to perceive and define relationships, sequence events, and form inferences. But beyond the academic world, students will find logical thinking an integral part of everyday life. These are the skills that allow students to analyze situations, see relationships, organize information, and draw generalizations. As students develop their logical thinking skills, expect them to approach all information with critical forethought.

The activities in this book were created for working with small groups or with individual students. These activities fall into eight broad categories:

- relationships
- analogies
- sequences
- syllogisms
- deduction
- inference
- logical reasoning
- logical notation.

The instructor's role

The instructor is the most important element for making logic interesting and stimulating to young thinkers. It is the instructor's role to not only present the process for solving the puzzles but also to build an atmosphere that encourages analytical thinking. Since the thought process itself is more valuable than the answers listed in the back of the book, it is very important to compare and discuss methods of arriving at conclusions and to be tolerant of creative diversions from the norm. Though the material in this book is presented in a sequential manner, it is suggested that each new type of logic problem be presented and discussed and sample problems be worked together before students are allowed to work independently. By discussing the puzzles, students will be able to learn a generalized thinking process instead of having to tackle each problem as a unique entity.

Other books in this series

Logic Liftoff is the second in the three-part series of logic books for students in grades three through seven. Logical skills are developed in a sequential, developmental fashion by these three books. Concepts introduced in one book are reinforced by the next book while new skills are added. Students begin their adventures with *Logic Countdown*. If students are unfamiliar with logical thinking, it is advisable to introduce them to some of the exercises in *Logic Countdown* before moving on to the other two books. Then they can move on to new challenges with *Logic Liftoff* before they sharpen their reasoning abilities even more with *Orbiting with Logic*. Together the three books provide an entertaining, sequenced experience in logical thinking.

Specific information on logical thinking skills

Relationships

In this section, students will be looking for ways that certain things are related. The relationship is not always obvious, so students must be flexible in their thinking. When the obvious relationship does not hold up, they should look for other, less obvious, similarities.

Analogies

This section contains exercises in both figural or pictorial analogies and literal analogies. Analogies are a comparison between two things. In order to be able to solve analogies, students must first be familiar with relationships. To solve the analogy, students must look for the relationship between the first two items and then establish the same relationship between the other two things in the analogy. The choices for answers are usually closely related to the first member of the second set, but students must make sure that the word they choose is not only related, but related in the same way that the first two members of the analogy are related.

For example, red : color :: shirt : garment

          red : apple :: sharp : knife

          red : pink :: purple : mauve

          red : snapper :: blue : whale

Deduction

Deduction is a form of inferencing in which the conclusion follows from the premises or statements of fact. It involves going from the general to the specific. Deduction problems in this book give students information concerning a situation and ask them to solve the puzzle by logically linking together all of the facts. It requires making connections between the related bits of information by combining, relating, ordering, and eliminating. Students must look at each clue individually and also in relation to other clues in order to derive as much information as possible.

Sequences

Sequencing problems, like other problems in this book, require students to look at relationships. In this case, students are presented with a series and asked to look for the relationship between the members of the series and then to select the next member. In some of the easier problems, the relationship is a static one, and in harder problems, the relationship itself is a sequence.

Example

2, 4, 6, 8, 10... This is an arithmetic sequence (add 2).

1, 5, 25, 125, 625... This is a geometric sequence (multiply by 5).

2, 10, 12, 60, 62, 310, 312... This is a combination sequence (add 2, multiply by 5).

2, 4, 7, 11, 16,... This is a changing arithmetic sequence (add 2, add 3, add 4).

As students work these problems, they will encounter a variety of sequential patterns. To solve the problems, they must look carefully at the relationships that have been established in the sequence. To do this, they should remain flexible in their thinking, looking at the sequence from many different perspectives.

Syllogisms

Syllogisms are one of the oldest logic arguments. These problems always contain at least two statements that are called premises and one statement that is called the conclusion. In its simplest form, the syllogism is stated:

    All A are B.

    All B are C.

    Therefore, all A are C.

Instead of "all," syllogisms may also have premises that use the words "some" or "no."

If the premises support the conclusion, the syllogism is said to be valid. If the conclusion cannot be supported by the premises, the syllogism is said to be invalid.

Example: All roses are flowers. (premise)

          All flowers are pretty. (premise)

          Therefore, all roses are pretty. (conclusion)

          This is a valid argument.

The premises of the syllogism do not have to be true, and can, in fact, be nonsensical. They do, however, have to establish a relationship that will support the conclusion.

In the exercises in this book, students will work with syllogisms that are formed from "all" statements, "some" statements, and "no" statements. They will be asked to select the valid conclusion as well as to write valid conclusions. In order to solve these problems, students should be encouraged to read carefully and, if necessary, draw a graphic representation of the syllogism.

Inferences

Inferencing is a broad area of logic. Inferencing involves reaching conclusions from gathered evidence. It means going from the known to the unknown and forming educated guesses based on either facts or premises. If the information is in the form of premises and the conclusion follows from the premises, it is deductive inferencing. If the evidence is in the form of specific examples and the general principles are derived from the specific facts or instances, it is inductive inferencing.

This book includes several puzzle-type exercises to introduce students to inferential thinking. In all cases, students will be working with clues to solve the problem. They will also be introduced to inferential reasoning by determining if certain inferences are reasonable or not. In all cases, students should look critically at the evidence presented and try to go from there to the next reasonable step.

Logical Reasoning

Students will be briefly exposed to two areas of logical reasoning in addition to inferencing. These are relevant information and cause and effect. In both cases, students are asked to look at the information presented and determine if it can logically be applied to the situation. With these problems, as with the inferential reasoning problems, students should be encouraged to discuss their answers. They should be able to logically defend their answers.

Logical Notation

This section of the book deals with notation that is frequently used in logic problems. This notation forms an important part of the next book in this series, so students who master it in this book will be well-prepared to tackle the problems in the next book.

For reference, here is a brief summary of the concepts presented in the logical notation exercises.

1. A single thought can be represented by capital letters (either singly or in combination).
   R can stand for "The rose is red."
   IP can stand for "I'll pick it."
2. An if-then statement can be written using → to represent "if-then" or "It implies."
   R → IP means "If the Rose is red, then I'll pick it."
3. The negation of a statement has the opposite truth value and is noted by ~ preceding the logical notation. A double negation is noted by ~~.
   ~R means "The rose is not red."   ~~R means "It is false that the rose is not red."
4. Two statements are equivalent if they can replace each other and have the same truth value. A statement is equivalent to itself and its double negation. The notation for equivalence is ≡.
   R ≡ R
   R ≡ ~~R
5. Some logical statements have "and" or "or" in them. To negate an "and" statement, negate each part and change the "and" to "or." To negate an "or" statement, negate each part and change the "or" to "and."
   ~(A and B) ≡ ~A or ~B
   ~(A or B) ≡ ~A and ~B

Contents

Name_____

Use your reasoning ability to figure out what a hertog is.

These are hertogs.

 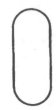 S

These are not hertogs.

Circle the things in this group that are hertogs.

1.    2.   3.   4.

5.   6.   7.   8.

9.   10.   11.   12.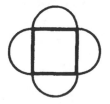

Describe the characteristics that make something a hertog.

_____

_____

Name_____

Use your reasoning ability to find out what a jayzel is.

These are jayzels.

 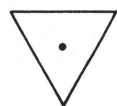 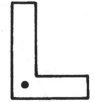 

These are not jayzels.

 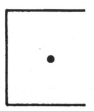   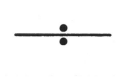

Circle the things in this group that are jayzels.

1.   2. 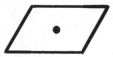   3.   4.

5.    6.   7.   8.

9.   10.   11.   12.

Describe the characteristics that make something a jayzel.

_____

_____

Name_____

Use your reasoning ability to find out what a notaddel is.

These are notaddels.

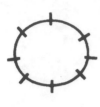 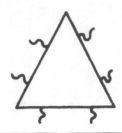  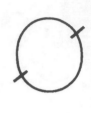

These are not notaddels.

 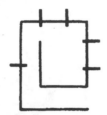 

Circle the things in this group that are notaddels.

1.    2.   3.    4.

5.   6. 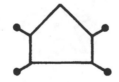   7.    8.

9. 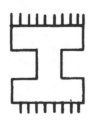   10.   11.   12.

Describe the characteristics that make something a notaddel.

_____

_____

Name_____

Use your reasoning ability to find out what a cinqueen is.

These are cinqueens.

    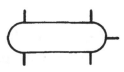

These are not cinqueens.

Circle the things in this group that are cinqueens.

1.   2.   3.   4.

5.   6.   7.   8.

9.    10.    11.   12.

Describe the characteristics that make something a cinqueen.

_____

_____

Name_____

Here are lists that describe people or the things they like. Look for the relationship between each of the things on the list. Write the common characteristic.

1. Penelope likes milk but not coffee.
   Penelope likes snow but not rain.
   Penelope likes polar bears but not sun bears.
   Penelope likes salt but not pepper.

   Penelope likes _____

2. Bill likes pepper but not salt.
   Bill likes cookies but not cake.
   Bill likes butter but not margarine.
   Bill likes jogging but not walking.

   Bill likes _____

3. Lisa likes Swiss cheese but not Cheddar cheese.
   Lisa likes doughnuts but not cookies.
   Lisa likes nuts but not bolts.
   Lisa likes needles but not pins.

   Lisa likes _____

4. Mike is chubby but not fat.
   Mike is clumsy but not awkward.
   Mike is clever but not smart.
   Mike is creative but not inventive.

   Mike is _____

5. Myra likes soccer but not golf.
   Myra likes reading but not math.
   Myra likes cookies but not cake.
   Myra likes skateboards but not bikes.

   Myra likes_____

6. Kate likes lakes but not puddles.
   Kate likes elephants but not ants.
   Kate likes trees but not shrubs.
   Kate likes mountains but not mole hills.

   Kate likes _____

Name_____

Analogies are comparisons between two things. They compare features that are not always obvious. Finish the following analogies by choosing the set of pictures or figures that best completes each sentence. Write the correct letter on the line.

_____ 1.   BƆD   is like   EꟻG   as

    a.   ƎꟻG   is like   HIL

    b.   ACE   is like   FHJ

    c.   IS3   is like   426

_____ 2.   ◼ is like ◼ as

    a.   ⊕ is like ◒

    b.   ◈ is like ◈

    c.   ⊠ is like ⊠

_____ 3.   □ is like □ as

    a.   △ is like ▲

    b.   ▭ is like ▯

    c.   ○ is like ○

_____ 4.   □○ is like ⊡ as

    a.   ○◇ is like ◇○

    b.   △☆ is like △☆

    c.   △○ is like △○

_____ 5.   □ is like ◼ as

    a.   △ is like △

    b.   □ is like ⊞

    c.   ▢ is like ▬

_____ 6.   L is like L as

    a.   is like

    b.   is like

    c.   is like

Name_____

Finish the following analogies by choosing the set of pictures or figures that best completes each sentence.

_____ 1. ◯ is like ☼ as

a. ◯ is like ⊛
b. ☐ is like ▢
c. ☐ is like ◼

_____ 2. ◯ is like ⌣ as

a. ☐ is like ⬠
b. △ is like ◢
c. ☐ is like ▦

_____ 3. ⬠ is like ⬠ as

a. △ is like ▽
b. ▭ is like ▥
c. ⊕ is like ◷

_____ 4. ⬭ is like ◯ as

a. ▭ is like ☐
b. ▭ is like ▨
c. ⬭ is like ▢

_____ 5. ◭ is like △◯ as

a. ▢△ is like ◸△
b. ▢△ is like ▢☐
c. ◬ is like ◭●

_____ 6. ◯ is like ⊕ as

a. ◮ is like ⬠
b. ☐ is like ◼
c. △ is like ◬

Name_____

Finish the following statements by choosing the word that best completes each
analogy. Consider carefully the relationship between the first two members of
the analogy. Then look for the same relationship between the second two
members of the analogy. Write the letter of the correct answer in the space.

Example grape : vine :: apple : tree

1. gallon : quart :: hour : _____
   a. clock
   b. day
   c. time
   d. minute

2. see : behold :: distinct : _____
   a. fuzzy
   b. vague
   c. clear
   d. disturb

3. beagle : dalmatian ::
   appaloosa : _____
   a. horse
   b. palomino
   c. herd
   d. stallion

4. penthouse : skyscraper ::
   summit : _____
   a. climb
   b. peak
   c. mountain
   d. snow

5. tribe : Sioux :: cheese : _____
   a. milk
   b. mouse
   c. age
   d. Cheddar

6. mirror : looking glass ::
   disappear : _____
   a. vanish
   b. appear
   c. reflection
   d. magic

7. spoon : spoons :: elf : _____
   a. fairy
   b. leprechaun
   c. tiny
   d. elves

8. snow : skiing :: ice : _____
   a. cold
   b. slick
   c. hockey
   d. frozen

9. noise : silence ::
   steadfast : _____
   a. steady
   b. soldier
   c. quiet
   d. unreliable

10. child : skip :: duckling : _____
    a. ugly
    b. egg
    c. waddle
    d. downy

11. beige : brown :: mauve : _____
    a. gray
    b. light
    c. purple
    d. color

12. cotton : fabric ::
    schooner : _____
    a. sailing
    b. wooden
    c. scorpion
    d. ship

Name_____

Finish the following statements by choosing the word that best completes each analogy. Consider carefully the relationship between the first two members of the analogy. Then look for the same relationship between the second two members of the analogy.

Example afar : near :: beautiful : ugly

1. silence : stillness ::
   examine : _____
   a. inspect
   b. doctor
   c. teeth
   d. failure

2. basket : straw :: vase :
   _____
   a. pitcher
   b. flower
   c. cracked
   d. ceramic

3. piano : violin ::
   cantaloupe : _____
   a. slice
   b. seed
   c. watermelon
   d. vine

4. roof : house :: crest :
   _____
   a. climb
   b. hill
   c. crust
   d. fall

5. solution : answer :: test :
   _____
   a. spelling
   b. difficult
   c. trial
   d. tests

6. planet : Venus :: fruit :
   _____
   a. vegetable
   b. harvest
   c. tree
   d. banana

7. tolerant : prejudiced ::
   indifferent : _____
   a. boy
   b. curious
   c. different
   d. time

8. owl : owls :: louse : _____
   a. loose
   b. mouse
   c. lose
   d. lice

9. ant : colony :: outlaw :
   _____
   a. gang
   b. crime
   c. sheriff
   d. lawyer

10. kite : fly :: wagon : _____
    a. wheel
    b. horse
    c. roll
    d. bike

11. mold : shape :: inhabit :
    _____
    a. moldy
    b. inhibit
    c. reside
    d. habit

12. initial : last :: obnoxious :
    _____
    a. orthodox
    b. pleasant
    c. disagreeable
    d. punishment

14

Name_____

Finish the following statements by choosing the word that best completes each
analogy. Consider carefully the relationship between the first two members of
the analogy. Then look for the same relationship between the second two
members of the analogy.

Example three : triangle :: five : pentagon

1. chance : risk :: reliable :

____
a. help
b. dare
c. driver
d. dependable

2. Mississippi : river ::
petunia : ____
a. flower
b. garden
c. violet
d. purple

3. pear : apple :: blond :

____
a. girl
b. hair
c. brunette
d. curl

4. brief : lengthy :: comedy :

____
a. laugh
b. funny
c. slapstick
d. tragedy

5. carpenter : saw :: judge :

____
a. lawyer
b. gavel
c. decision
d. courtroom

6. bewildered : perplexed ::
vague : ____
a. chicken
b. vogue
c. happy
d. unclear

7. flowers : flower :: axes :

____
a. hatchet
b. chop
c. trees
d. ax

8. kangaroo : mob ::
aborigine : ____
a. tribe
b. hunt
c. spear
d. abnormal

9. fork : silver :: table :

____
a. chair
b. kitchen
c. leg
d. mahogany

10. serene : excited :: north :

____
a. south
b. pole
c. snow
d. west

11. editorial : newspaper ::
verse : ____
a. opinion
b. poem
c. comics
d. version

12. regatta : boats :: meet :

____
a. meeters
b. swimmers
c. competition
d. parting

15

Name_____

Finish the following statements by choosing the word that best completes each analogy. Consider carefully the relationship between the first two members of the analogy. Then look for the same relationship between the second two members of the analogy.

Example thing : noun :: action : verb

1. grove : tree :: pride :
   _____
   a. Africa
   b. lion
   c. hunt
   d. mane

2. nation : Australia ::
   illness : _____
   a. sickness
   b. measles
   c. fever
   d. clinic

3. blue : purple :: pie : _____
   a. bake
   b. sweet
   c. lemon
   d. cake

4. shoe : shoes :: baby :
   _____
   a. infant
   b. cry
   c. babies
   d. bottle

5. scissors : barber ::
   tractor : _____
   a. plant
   b. field
   c. farmer
   d. plow

6. wager : bet :: genuine :
   _____
   a. gem
   b. content
   c. authentic
   d. counterfeit

7. leather : purse :: wool :
   _____
   a. knit
   b. sheep
   c. nylon
   d. sweater

8. first : final :: funny : _____
   a. joke
   b. comic
   c. tickle
   d. sad

9. closet : coat :: pantry :
   _____
   a. book
   b. potato
   c. sweater
   d. larder

10. redwood : spruce ::
    reindeer : _____
    a. snow
    b. Santa Claus
    c. antelope
    d. leap

11. classical : music :: ballet :
    : _____
    a. slipper
    b. graceful
    c. company
    d. dance

12. kangaroo : marsupial ::
    bamboo : _____
    a. tropics
    b. grass
    c. Australian
    d. bamboozle

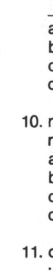

Name_____

Finish the following statements by choosing the word that best completes each analogy. Consider carefully the relationship between the first two members of the analogy. Then look for the same relationship between the second two members of the analogy.

Example excavate : shovel :: navigate : compass

1. dispatch : send :: taxi :
   ____
   a. street
   b. driver
   c. fare
   d. cab

2. plastic : beach ball ::
   concrete : ____
   a. hard
   b. solid
   c. patio
   d. rocks

3. clay : silt :: barley : ____
   a. barely
   b. grow
   c. millet
   d. field

4. fireman : hose :: catcher :
   ____
   a. pitcher
   b. mitt
   c. outfield
   d. slide

5. transport : convey ::
   mariner : ____
   a. ancient
   b. ocean
   c. sailor
   d. ship

6. star : constellations ::
   gnat : ____
   a. swarm
   b. pest
   c. fruit
   d. nap

7. coin : dime :: music :
   ____
   a. play
   b. sound
   c. note
   d. rock 'n roll

8. ornamentation :
   simplicity :: modesty :
   ____
   a. vanity
   b. girl
   c. model
   d. man

9. bears : bear :: leaves :
   ____
   a. rake
   b. fall
   c. tree
   d. leaf

10. refrigerator : kitchen ::
    typewriter : ____
    a. ribbon
    b. office
    c. paper
    d. typist

11. tachometer : speed ::
    barometer : ____
    a. temperature
    b. weather
    c. bars
    d. atmospheric pressure

12. barrister : law :: thespian
    : ____
    a. drama
    b. defendent
    c. audience
    d. poetry

Name_____

Finish the following statements by choosing the word that best completes each analogy. Consider carefully the relationship between the first two members of the analogy. Then look for the same relationship between the second two members of the analogy.

Example menace : troublesome :: assistant : helpful

1. tire : rubber :: street :
   _____
   a. avenue
   b. puncture
   c. asphalt
   d. lane

2. furrow : groove :: tranquil
   :_____
   a. excited
   b. serene
   c. swan
   d. quilt

3. Idaho : state :: bicycle :
   _____
   a. brake
   b. pedal
   c. vehicle
   d. rack

4. Catholic : church ::
   lobster : _____
   a. ocean
   b. crab
   c. broiled
   d. crustacean

5. knowledge : ignorance ::
   gamble : _____
   a. dice
   b. risk
   c. cards
   d. certainty

6. measuring cup : chef ::
   goggles : _____
   a. cook
   b. glass
   c. diver
   d. geese

7. chasm : gulf :: velocity :
   _____
   a. velour
   b. sad
   c. speed
   d. velvet

8. eye : eyes :: man : _____
   a. son
   b. men
   c. guy
   d. fellow

9. newsprint : paper ::
   tweed : _____
   a. help
   b. two
   c. weed
   d. fabric

10. Cairn terrier : Irish setter
    :: cypress : _____
    a. duck
    b. knee
    c. elm
    d. swamp

11. inhale : breathe :: ingest :
    _____
    a. gestation
    b. lungs
    c. swallow
    d. living

12. beetle : insect :: platypus
    : _____
    a. mammal
    b. fish
    c. marsupial
    d. duck

Name_____

Finish the following statements by choosing the word that best completes each analogy. Consider carefully the relationship between the first two members of the analogy. Then look for the same relationship between the second two members of the analogy.
Example ten : decade :: one hundred : century.

1. wig : toupee :: spine : _____
   a. posture
   b. backbone
   c. orthopedics
   d. flexible

2. cardboard : box :: silk : _____
   a. worm
   b. weave
   c. blouse
   d. oriental

3. ruby : emerald :: Danish : _____
   a. pastry
   b. ham
   c. Icelandic
   d. diamond

4. child : children :: hat : _____
   a. brim
   b. cap
   c. hats
   d. beret

5. sharp : keen :: cut : _____
   a. sword
   b. slice
   c. knife
   d. scissors

6. awl : cobbler :: rope : _____
   a. twine
   b. jute
   c. sailor
   d. hemp

7. city : Omaha :: weed : _____
   a. herbicide
   b. hoe
   c. crabgrass
   d. garden

8. fragrance : stench :: tarnished : _____
   a. andiron
   b. silver
   c. polished
   d. brass

9. topaz : garnet :: hibiscus : _____
   a. jonquil
   b. flower
   c. petal
   d. blossom

10. hickory : maple :: Parmesan : _____
    a. cheese
    b. Cheddar
    c. milk
    d. goat

11. hydrogen : water :: sodium : _____
    a. oxygen
    b. salt
    c. carbon dioxide
    d. mineral

12. smooth : rough :: stingy : _____
    a. president   c. stringy
    b. generous   d. cheap

Name_____

The following sets are in a logical sequence. Examine each set carefully and choose the item that should logically be the next item in the set. Write the correct answer on the line.

Example 1, 2, 3, _4_
a. 5 b. 2 c. 4 d. 6

1. 2, 4, 6, _____
   a. 7 b. 5 c. 10 d. 8

2. ab, bc, cd, _____
   a. ef b. de c. ed d. fg

3. 105, 107, 110, 112, _____
   a. 116 b. 115 c. 114 d. 109

4. 1/2, 1/3, 1/4, _____
   a. 1/5 b. 1/6 c. 2/4 d. 2/3

5. kl, mn, op, _____
   a. pq b. on c. qr d. rs

6. 1, 5, 2, 10, 3, _____
   a. 4 b. 30 c. 25 d. 15

7. July 31, June 30 , May 31, _____
   a. April 30 b. December 31
   c. March 31 d. August 31

8. 1987, 1985, 1983, _____
   a. 1984 b. 1980 c. 1981 d. 1982

9. 560, 56.0, 5.60, _____
   a. 0560 b. .560 c. 56.0 d. 560.0

10. 1/8, 1/4, 3/8, _____
    a. 3/9 b. 5/8 c. 3/7 d. 1/2

11. it, fit, fist, _____
    a. tif b. first c. flit d. is

12. triangle, quadrilateral, pentagon,

    _____

    a. hexagon b. polygon c. octagon
    d. decahedron

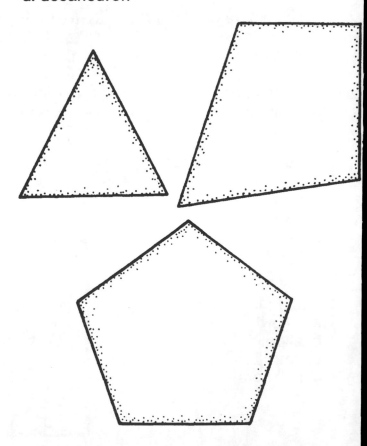

20

Name_____

The following sets are in a logical sequence. Examine each set carefully and choose the item that should logically be the next item in the set. Write the correct answer on the line.

Example 82, 84, 86, __*88*__

a. 80   b. 88   c. 87   d. 90

1. uni, bi, tri, _____
   a. quad   b. quin   c. octa   d. hexa

2. 20, 21, 23, 26, _____
   a. 28   b. 29   c. 30   d. 31

3. 20, 30, 39, 47, _____
   a. 53   b. 54   c. 55   d. 50

4. 1, 4, 9, 16, _____
   a. 26   b. 36   c. 20   d. 25

5. 100, 99, 97, 94, _____
   a. 93   b. 90   c. 92   d. 91

6. 5, 25, 125, _____
   a. 250   b. 625   c. 550   d. 455

7. I, III, V, _____
   a. VII   b. V   c. VI   d. IX

8. 4$\frac{4}{5}$, 5$\frac{5}{6}$, 6$\frac{6}{7}$, _____
   a. 8$\frac{7}{8}$ b. 7$\frac{7}{8}$ c. 9$\frac{9}{7}$ d. 9$\frac{9}{9}$

9. January, 1, March, 3, May, 5, _____
   a. August, 8   b. June, 7   c. July, 7
   d. July, 6

10. 2, 6, 18, 54, _____
    a. 90   b. 108   c. 72   d. 162

11. Abe, Beth, Christopher, Doris, _____
    a. Ellen   b. Frank   c. Kim   d. Ethan

12. 8:10, 8:15, 8:20 _____
    a. 9:30   b. 8:30   c. 8:25   d. 8:45

Name ____________________

The following sets are in a logical sequence which has been interrupted at regular intervals by a repeating non-member of the set. Examine each set carefully and choose the item that should logically follow. Write the answer on the line.

Example 1, 9, 2, 9, 3, 9, __4__
a. 9 b. 5 c. 2 d. 4

1. 10, 11, 20, 11, 30, ________
   a. 11 b. 40 c. 50 d. 35

2. Monday, Friday, Tuesday, Friday, Wednesday, ________
   a. Thursday b. Friday c. Saturday d. Monday

3. f, e, g, e, h, e, ________
   a. e b. l c. i d. f

4. $\frac{1}{2}$, $\frac{1}{3}$, $\frac{1}{8}$, $\frac{1}{4}$, $\frac{1}{5}$, $\frac{1}{8}$, ________
   a. $\frac{2}{3}$ b. $\frac{1}{6}$ c. $\frac{2}{8}$ d. $\frac{2}{5}$

5. 4, 5, 3, 6, 7, 3, ________
   a. 4 b. 9 c. 3 d. 8

6. z, w, y, w, x, w, ________
   a. y b. w c. u d. v

7. 5, 0, 9, 0, 13, ________
   a. 6 b. 9 c. 0 d. 8

8. hi, n, ij, n, jk, n, ________
   a. kl b. nn c. on d. op

9. 100, 75, 90, 75, 80, 75, ________
   a. 85 b. 60 c. 65 d. 70

10. .005, 7, 0.05, 7, 00.5, 7, ________
    a. .07 b. 0.7 c. 005. d. 7.0

11. ace, abc, bdf, abc, ceg, abc, dfh, abc, ________
    a. efh b. fhj c. egi d. eca

12. $\frac{1}{2}$, $\frac{1}{4}$, $\frac{1}{2}$, $\frac{1}{6}$, $\frac{1}{2}$, $\frac{1}{8}$, $\frac{1}{2}$, ________
    a. $\frac{1}{16}$ b. $\frac{1}{10}$ c. $\frac{2}{8}$ d. $\frac{1}{12}$

Name_____

Here are thirteen parts of a story called "The Move." However, the statements are not listed in proper sequence. Read the statements carefully to determine in what order they should appear. Number the statements to indicate the correct order.

_____ It rained Monday afternoon and Michelle stayed in her room looking at old yearbooks and thinking how unfair it was that two friends as close as Lisa and she should be separated.

_____ Michelle found her mother in the kitchen. "That was your father. He's already at the airport. I want you to finish the chicken on the grill, make a salad, put the potatoes in the microwave at exactly 6:30, and take the pie out of the oven when the buzzer goes off." Her mother gave her a peck on the cheek and added, "And for goodness sake try to put on a smile before Dad sees you."

_____ Her dad gave her a big hug. He could usually cheer her up, but he brought only a slight smile to her face.

___1___ Monday morning Michelle stood upstairs in her room and watched the moving van roll away from the house next door. Lisa had been her best friend since second grade. Now she was gone, moving with her family to North Carolina.

_____ Tuesday Michelle's mother forced her to go to the pool with Juanita and Bev. Other friends were nice, but no one could ever be as close and share as many secrets as Lisa. They'd taken swimming lessons together at this very pool.

_____ Michelle returned from an afternoon at the pool more glum than ever. After her shower, she curled up on her bed and fell asleep.

_____ "I'll never like them," though Michelle stubbornly as she watched the movers carrying in couches and tables.

_____ She turned over intending to go back to sleep when her mom yelled, "Michelle, I need you downstairs."

_____ After the homecoming dinner, the family watched a humorous movie on the VCR.

_____ Friday morning Michelle walked outside to retrieve her father's newspaper when a boy slightly older than her said, "Hi, neighbor." Michelle finally smiled.

_____ The ringing of the phone woke her from her nap.

_____ Michelle had just prepared a salad when she heard the family car in the garage.

_____ It was Thursday when the second moving van arrived next door.

23

Name_____

Here are twelve parts of a story called "The Sleep Over." However, the statements are not listed in proper sequence. Read the statements carefully to determine in what order they should appear. Number the statements to indicate the correct order.

_____ Margo showed Mrs. Chan, the driver, her permission slip to ride bus 29 to Sandy's house.

_____ After dinner the girls and Ryan went for a swim in the back yard pool while Mrs. Pierson drove to the airport to pick up her husband.

_____ Mr. and Mrs. Pierson arrived home during the spookiest part of the film. Margo threw her popcorn into the air when the back door suddenly opened. The girls were relieved when Sandy's father shouted, "We're home."

_____ Margo's mom came to pick her up Saturday afternoon.

__1__ Sandy and Margo could hardly keep their minds on Mr. Crawford's Friday current events class. They were both anticipating the sleep over that evening at Sandy's house.

_____ Margo made microwave popcorn while Sandy carried her sleeping brother upstairs to bed.

_____ At 11 p.m. Mr. and Mrs. Pierson told the girls good night and went upstairs to bed.

_____ At 4 a.m. Mr. Pierson told the girls to turn off the stereo and go to bed.

_____ After the dismissal bell, the girls met at their lockers.

_____ At eight the swimmers dried off and changed clothes. While the girls watched a spooky movie, Ryan fell asleep on the couch.

_____ Margo and Sandy slept through breakfast and only got up when Ryan and Bosco, the family St. Bernard, pounced on their bed.

_____ Mr. Pierson, Sandy's father, was out of town so Sandy's mom took the girls and Ryan, her little brother, out for tacos and burritos for dinner.

Name_____

Here are nine parts of a story called "The Blizzard." However, the statements are not listed in proper sequence. Read the statements carefully to determine in what order they should appear. Number the statements to indicate the correct order.

_____ He turned up his jacket collar and pulled his hat low against the blustering wind. The snow had been falling now for over an hour, the prairie landmarks he'd studied so carefully were completely blanketed, and Lee was hopelessly lost.

_____ Back in Missouri they had plenty of timber for fuel. But all spring and summer here in Kansas, Pearl and Mae, the younger girls, had gathered dried buffalo chips that burned with a steady intense heat for cook fires. But with the herds migrating and winter approaching, the family must have a dependable fuel supply. It had been at least three hours now since Lee had given the oxen their head.

__1__ It was late morning as Lee watched the angry clouds push rapidly from the west and remembered the warning of the old man at the depot. "Better put up here over night," he said. "Bad storm comin'."

_____ He had stopped trying to guide the pair of oxen over an hour ago. His nose and toes and ears had stopped aching now. He tried not to think about death. He tried not to remember the old-timer's warnings about prairie storms.

_____ He remembered that earlier that morning he had chuckled at the rail attendant's warning as he gazed up at the clear blue prairie sky.

_____ Lee, the oldest son, had been chosen to make the trip to the rail head for a wagon of coal. As Lee crouched on the wagon seat he became aware that the wagon had stopped. "Belle and Star must be lost too," he thought hopelessly.

_____ He gave his team encouragement as the snow was just beginning to fall. The sky was dark with clouds, although Lee knew it must be near midday.

_____ Lee climbed off the wagon to investigate why the oxen had halted. It was only then that he discovered steam rising from the pipe sticking up through the snow. It was a stove pipe, their own stove pipe. Belle and Star had stopped the wagon right on top of their dugout.

_____ After facing the prospect of freezing to death on the unfamiliar plains of their new home, Lee decided to give Belle and Star their head. Oxen were said to have an instinct to guide them through blizzards, dust storms, and darkness.

Name_____

One of the oldest of all logic problems, the syllogism, has three parts. The first two statements are called premises. The last statement is call the conclusion. A syllogism can be either valid (true) or invalid (false), depending on whether the conclusion is supported by the premises.

Example   All flowers smell good.
Violets are flowers.
Therefore, violets smell good.   Valid

All girls are females.
Some girls giggle.
Therefore, all females giggle   Invalid

Here are several premises and conclusions. Read each set carefully and decide if the syllogisms are valid or invalid. You may assume that the premises are true.

1. All basketball players can shoot baskets.
Bill is a player on the basketball team.
Therefore, Bill can shoot baskets.   valid   invalid

2. All ducks can swim.
Some ducks live in the zoo.
Therefore, the ducks in the zoo can swim.   valid   invalid

3. All vegetables are healthy.
Some vegetables are green.
Therefore, green things are healthy.   valid   invalid

4. No lions are purple.
All purple things giggle.
Therefore, all lions giggle.   valid   invalid

5. All students go to school.
People who go to school are smart.
Therefore, all students are smart.   valid   invalid

Name_____

In this exercise you will be given two premises and several conclusions. You may assume that the premises are true. Try decide if the conclusions that follow the premises are valid or invalid. After you decide if the conclusions can be supported by the premises, circle the correct answer.

All bluegill are fish.
All fish live in water.

1. Therefore, all fish have gills.   valid   invalid
2. Therefore, all fish are bluegills.   valid   invalid
3. Therefore, some bluegill have fins.   valid   invalid
4. Therefore, all bluegill live in water.   valid   invalid

All chipmunks are animals.
Animals are not plants

5. Therefore, no chipmunks are plants.   valid   invalid
6. Therefore, some chipmunks are plants.   valid   invalid
7. Therefore, no chipmunks have leaves.   valid   invalid
8. Therefore, some plants are chipmunks.   valid   invalid

All horses are fast.
All palominos are horses

9. Therefore, some palominos are pretty.   valid   invalid
10. Therefore, no palominos are fast.   valid   invalid
11. Therefore, all palominos are fast.   valid   invalid

All cats are cunning.
All Cheshires are cats.

12. Therefore, all Cheshires are cunning.   valid   invalid
13. Therefore, all cunning animals are cats.   valid   invalid
14. Therefore, all cunning animals are Cheshires. valid   invalid

Name_____

In this exercise you will be given two premises and several conclusions. You may assume that the premises are true. Try to decide if the conclusions that follow the premises are valid or invalid. After you decide if the conclusions are supported by the premises, circle the correct answer.

All blondes have blue eyes.
Jackie is blonde.

1. Therefore, Jackie has blue eyes.	valid	invalid
2. Therefore, all blue-eyed people are blondes.	valid	invalid
3. Therefore, all blondes are named Jackie.	valid	invalid

All bears love honey.
All cubs are bears.

4. Therefore, all cubs love honey.	valid	invalid
5. Therefore, all animals that love honey are bears.	valid	invalid
6. Therefore, all animals that love honey are cubs.	valid	invalid

No snake can read.
All boa constrictors are snakes.

7. Therefore, all snakes are boa constrictors.	valid	invalid
8. Therefore, no snakes own books.	valid	invalid
9. Therefore, boa constrictors cannot read.	valid	invalid

All eagles are birds.
All birds have feathers.

10. Therefore, all eagles can fly.	valid	invalid
11. Therefore, all eagles have feathers.	valid	invalid
12. Therefore, some birds eat rabbits.	valid	invalid
13. Therefore, all eagles have talons.	valid	invalid

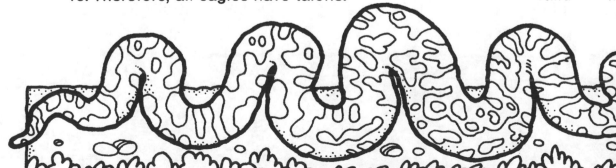

Name_____

In this exercise you will be given two premises and several conclusions. You may assume that the premises are true. Try to decide if the conclusions that follow the premises are valid or invalid. After you decide if the conclusions are supported by the premises, circle the correct answer.

All dragons have scales.
All things with scales are green.
　1. Therefore, all dragons are green.　　　　　　valid　　　invalid
　2. Therefore, all green things are dragons.　　　valid　　　invalid
　3. Therefore, some dragons are scarey.　　　　　valid　　　invalid
　4. Therefore, no dragons are pink.　　　　　　　valid　　　invalid

No horses can fly.
All mustangs are horses.
　5. Therefore, some mustangs can fly.　　　　　　valid　　　invalid
　6. Therefore, all mustangs can fly.　　　　　　　valid　　　invalid
　7. Therefore, no mustangs can fly.　　　　　　　valid　　　invalid
　8. Therefore, nothing that flies is a mustang.　　valid　　　invalid

All dolls are cuddly.
Some toys are dolls.
　9. Therefore, all toys are dolls.　　　　　　　　valid　　　invalid
10. Therefore, some toys are cuddly.　　　　　　　valid　　　invalid
11. Therefore, some toys say "mama."　　　　　　valid　　　invalid

No gurks are purple.
All fribbles are purple.
12. Therefore, all gurks are fribbles.　　　　　　valid　　　invalid
13. Therefore, no gurks are fribbles.　　　　　　valid　　　invalid
14. Therefore, all purple things are gurks.　　　　valid　　　invalid

Name _____

Each set has two premises. Assume that the premises are true. Write one valid conclusion for the two premises.

1. All whales are mammals.
   Mammals give live birth.
   Therefore, _____

2. No reptiles are warm-blooded.
   Lizards are reptiles.
   Therefore, _____

3. All mice have tails.
   Mickey is a mouse.
   Therefore, _____

4. No ducks can bark.
   Donald is a duck.
   Therefore, _____

5. All crooks are dishonest.
   No dishonest people are happy.
   Therefore, _____

6. All skiers like snow.
   George likes to ski.
   Therefore, _____

7. All frogs were once tadpoles.
   All tadpoles hatched from eggs.
   Therefore, _____

8. All arachnids have eight legs.
   Spiders are arachnids.
   Therefore, _____

9. All water contains oxygen.
   Ice is a form of water.
   Therefore, _____

10. All gumps are green.
    All green things are slimy.
    Therefore, _____

11. All herbivores eat plants.
    No lions eat plants.
    Therefore, _____

12. All free things are blue.
    No blue things are fleebles.
    Therefore, _____

13. All even numbers are divisible by two.
    276,454 is an even number.
    Therefore, _____

Name _____

Each set has two premises. Assume that the premises are true. Write one valid conclusion for the two premises.

1. No mountains are small.
   Everest is a mountain.
   Therefore, _____

2. All clowns are funny.
   Freckles is a clown.
   Therefore, _____

3. All children are adorable.
   Some children are boys.
   Therefore, _____

4. No cats are purple.
   All prickly things are purple.
   Therefore, _____

5. All cows eat grass.
   All grass-eaters are part of the food chain.
   Therefore, _____

6. All insects are scary.
   All scary things frighten me.
   Therefore, _____

7. All rabbits are herbivores.
   All herbivores eat plants.
   Therefore, _____

8. All machines make work easier.
   A lawn mower is a machine.
   Therefore, _____

Write your own syllogisms. Each one should include two premises and a conclusion that is supported by the premises.

9. _____
   _____
   _____

10. _____
    _____
    _____

Name _____

The Stadium

Joe and his father went to the stadium to see a baseball game. Joe noticed six team banners along the outfield wall. The banners were from the St. Louis Cardinals, New Yok Mets, Montreal Expos, Philadelphia Phillies, Chicago Cubs, and Pittsburgh Pirates. Read the clues below to find out where each banner was hanging.

Clues
1. The Phillies' banner was left of the Cubs' banner and to the right of the Mets' banner.
2. The Cardinals', Pirates', and Expos' banners were in right field.
3. The Expos' and Pirates' banners were not next to the Cubs' banner.
4. The Pirates' banner was not on the end.

Name_____

The Book Shelf

There are six books on the shelf in Steven's room—*Tom Sawyer, Old Yeller, Kidnapped, Robinson Crusoe, Gulliver's Travels,* and *Savage Sam.* Steven likes the books arranged in a certain order. The books are different colors. One is red, one is black, one is blue, and three are brown. Use the clues to help you find the order and color of the books on the shelf.

Clues
1. *Old Yeller* and *Savage Sam* are by the same author but are not side by side or the same color.
2. *Kidnapped* is to the right of *Old Yeller* and the blue book but to the left of the brown books.
3. *Savage Sam* is to the right of one brown book and *Kidnapped* but to the left of *Tom Sawyer.*
4. The book to the far left is red.
5. *Gulliver's Travels* is not next to the red book.

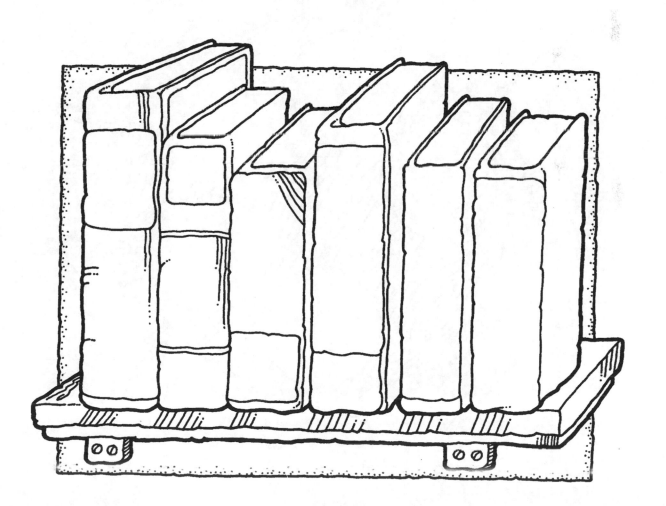

Name_____

The Round Table

Ken, Maggie, Jolie, Drew, and Bob went to the Round Table for lunch. Each person ordered something different—chicken nuggets, fish sandwich, quarter-pound cheeseburger, roast beef sandwich, and a taco salad. Use the clues to determine what each person ordered and where they sat.

Clues
1. Maggie sat between the boy who ordered chicken nuggets and Bob.
2. Ken and the girl who ordered the roast beef sandwich both sat next to the empty chair.
3. Bob sat between the girl ordering the taco salad and Drew.
4. The boy with the cheeseburger was seated to Drew's right and Jolie was seated to Drew's left.

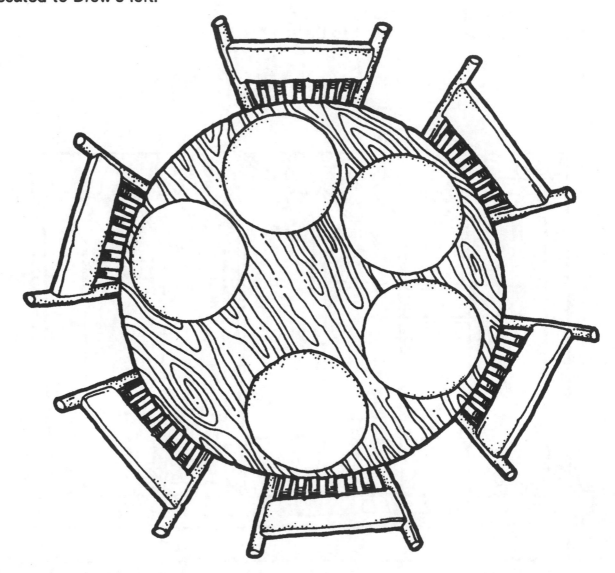

Name_____

The Snow Cone Man

Brian, Andrew, Mike, and Robby play together in the summer. When they hear the Snow Cone Man's bell, they run to ask their mothers if they may buy a cone. The boys are 9, 10, 10½, and 11 years old. Each friend likes a different flavor: grape, cherry, blueberry, and orange. Read the clues to find out each boy's age and favorite flavor of snow cone.

Clues

1. Andrew is older than Mike and the boy who likes blueberry but younger than the boy who likes orange.
2. The boy who likes blueberry is the youngest.
3. Brian and Andrew do not like grape.
4. Brian is not the oldest.

Name_____

Webster Hills Bath and Tennis Club

Brendan, Catherine, Donald, Suzanne, and Paul (whose last names are Becker, Cowell, Graham, Ming, and Pearlstein) are life guards at Webster Hills Bath and Tennis Club. Their ages are 15, 16, 17, 18, and 18. Each person has a special position at the club. One person is swim team coach, one is diving coach, one is head life guard, one is assistant manager, and one is swim lessons instructor. Read the clues to determine the age, name, and special job of each person.

Clues
1. Brendan and Pearlstein are the same age.
2. Suzanne is older than Cowell and the boy who gives swimming lessons but younger than Ming and the boy who is assistant manager.
3. The girl who is diving coach is younger than Becker and the girl who is the swim team coach.
4. Paul is not Graham, the head life guard, or the assistant manager.

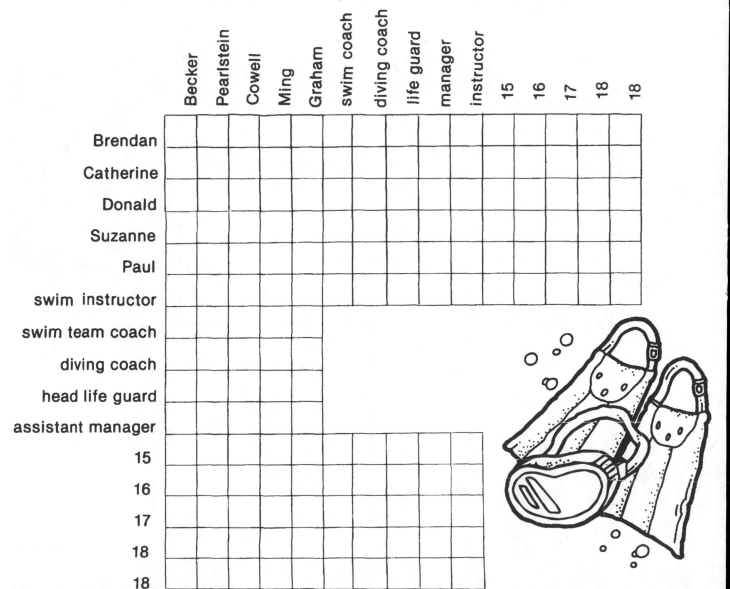

Name_____

The Fishing Contest

Four friends, Becky, Michelle, Jimmy, and Curt, entered a community fishing contest. Their last names are Cardwell, McDonnell, Brown, and Fisher. Each person chose a favorite bait. One person chose minnows, one chose crickets, and two used worms. Each friend won a different prize: first fish caught, most fish caught, biggest fish, and smallest fish. Use the clues to help you determine which bait each person chose and which prize he or she won.

Clues

1. Jimmy, Fisher, the girl who caught the most fish, and the girl who caught the smallest fish all arrived at the lake at 7 a.m.
2. Brown caught more fish than Michelle, the boy choosing crickets, or the boy choosing minnows.
3. Michelle, the boy using crickets, and Fisher all used bobbers.
4. Fisher caught the first fish at 7:04 a.m. using a minnow.
5. Michelle and McDonnell both got sunburned.

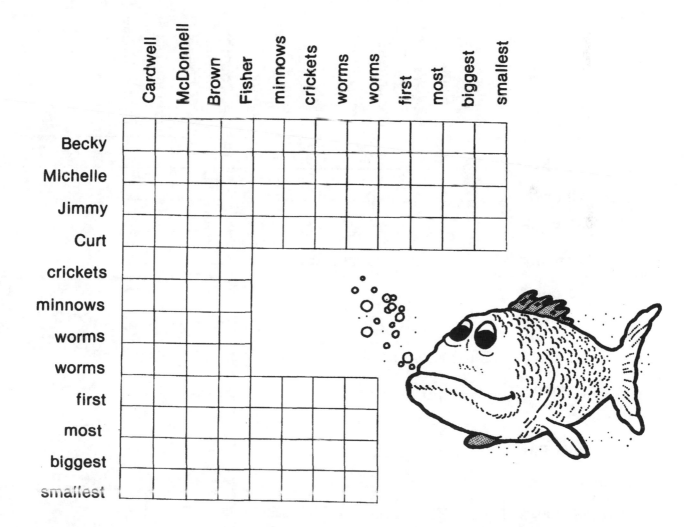

Name _____

The Zoo Trip

The sixth grade took a field trip to the zoo. Miss Busse appointed Ken, Kimberly, Brian, and Jennifer to be the leaders of the four groups. Each of the leaders had a different last name. The last names were Bouler, McCann, Roberts, and Dominguez. Each group also started their tour at a different location. One group started at Cat Country, one at Bear Pits, one at Primate House, and one at Reptile House. Use the clues to help you determine who lead each group and where they started their tours.

Clues
1. Ken, McCann, the boy who led group 2, and the girl whose group began at the Reptile House all had to keep track of the students in their group.
2. Dominguez, the girl who led group 3, the boy whose group began at the Bear Pits, and Jennifer all had a list of rules from Miss Busse.
3. Bouler led group 1 and started at the Reptile House.
4. Ken did not start at the Bear Pits or the Primate House.

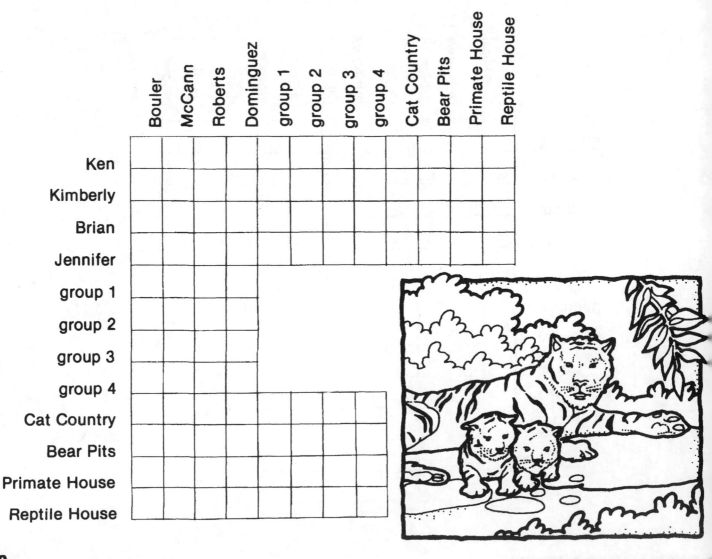

Name _____

Baby-sitting

Brian baby-sits for five children: Ashley, Robby, Sean, Casey, and Dana. Each of the children is a different age. The ages are 3 months, 9 months, 1 year, 2½ years, and 5 years. Each child also has a different bedtime. The bedtimes for the children are 6:00, 6:30, 7:00, 8:00, and 9:00 p.m. Use the clues to help you determine each child's age and bedtime.

Clues

1. Ashley and Robby are brother and sister, but Brian puts the baby to bed three hours after the 2½-year-old.
2. The oldest child goes to bed an hour after the 3-month-old and an hour before the 9-month-old.
3. Dana goes to bed half an hour later than Robby and a half an hour earlier than Sean.
4. Dana is older than Ashley and Sean but younger than Robby and Casey.
5. Ashley is not the youngest child.

Name _____

The Garage Sale

Jonathan, Monica, Tom, and Matthew went to a gargae sale where they each purchased a different item. They purchased a soccer net, a skateboard, a lighted mirror, and a broken clock. They spent $.50, $1.00, $2.50, and $2.75. The last names of the four friends are Baxter, Kincaid, Mano, and Staehle. Use the clues to help you discover what each person purchased at the garage sale and how much each person spent.

Clues
1. Jonathan, Staehle, the boy who bought the clock, and the boy who spent $2.75 all were excited about their purchases.
2. Jonathan spent more than Mano but less than the girl who bought the lighted mirror and the boy who bought the skateboard.
3. Staehle spent $2.00 more than Tom.
4. Matthew and Baxter are neighbors.

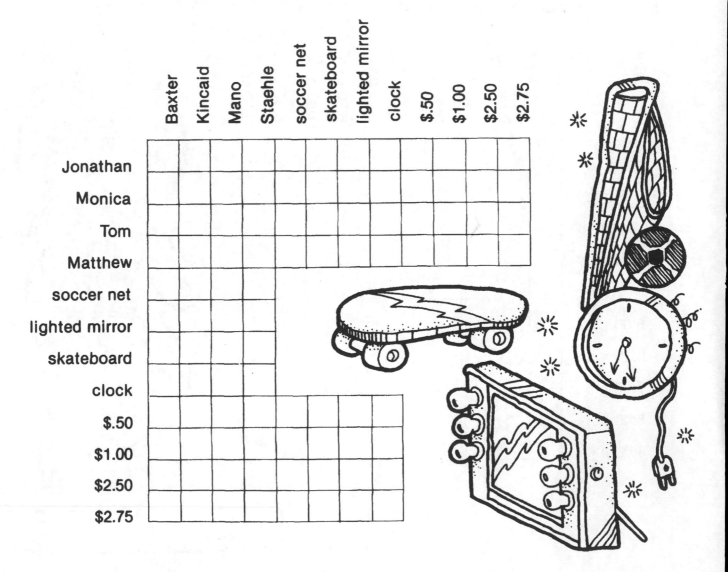

© Taylor & Francis Group. — **Logic Liftoff**

Name_____

Edy's Delicatessen

Bob, Candy, David, and Elvina have last names of Anastasi, Gerber, Rodriguez, and Reardon, and they all work at Edy's Delicatessen. Each person has a different shift that he or she is scheduled to work. One works Monday, Wednesday, and Friday. One works Wednesday and Friday. One works Tuesday, Thursday, and Saturday. One works Friday and Saturday. Two people are in 9th grade, one is in 10th grade, and one is in 11th grade. Use the clues to help you determine who works each shift and what grade each person is in.

Clues
1. Bob and Reardon are in the same grade.
2. Anastasi and Candy work together on Wednesday.
3. The boy in 9th grade, the girl in 9th grade, and Elvina are all scheduled to work on Friday.
4. Candy and the girl in 11th grade work fewer days than Rodriguez and Bob.

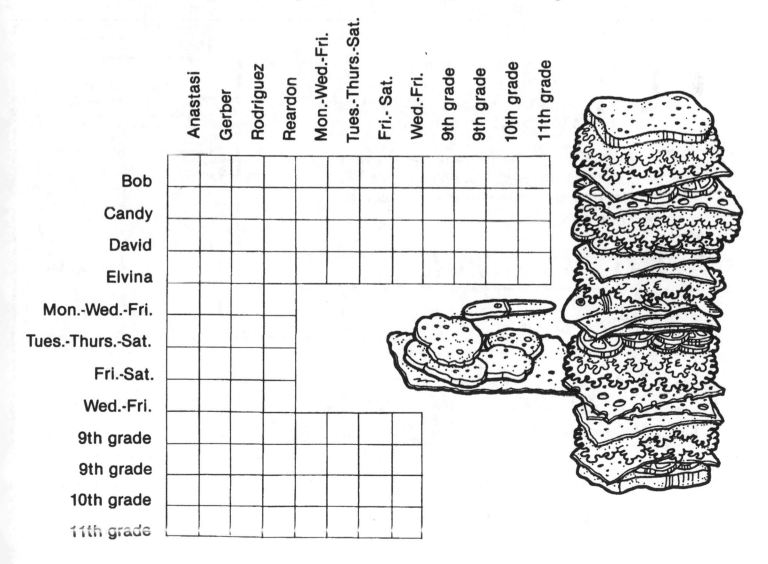

Name_____

Tell-Tale Footprints

Mrs. Morton wants to know which of her three children—Mikie, Julie, or Charles—left the muddy footprints on her clean floor. Read the following clues and see if you can solve the mystery.

1. At 5:00 Mrs. Morton came home to find muddy footprints on the kitchen floor.

2. Charles was wearing size 11 tennis shoes that were very dirty.

3. Julie and Mikie were seen playing in a mud puddle on their way home from school at 4:00, but Julie was wearing overshoes.

4. Julie was seen entering the house by the back door at 4:50, looking very guilty.

5. Mikie supplied cookies to all the children in the neighborhood at 4:30, from Mrs Morton's cookie jar.

6. Charles came home from basketball practice at 5:05.

7. Julie went to Janet's house to play instead of going home to practice her piano.

8. When Charles got home Julie was playing the piano and Mikie was not home. Julie's overshoes were sitting on the back porch and her shoes were clean.

9. None of the children came in or left the house except as stated in clues 1 to 8.

Solution _____

_____

_____

Name_____

Brown Bag Mystery

It's a mystery! Everyone would like to know what happend to Bianca's cookies. Read the following clues and see if you can find out what happened to the cookies.

1. An inspection at the lunch table showed that Carol had a bag of chocolate chip cookies in her lunch, but she said she did not take the cookies.

2. Bianca reported that her cookies were missing at the beginning of the lunch period.

3. Bianca found a tuna sandwich in her lunch.

4. Bianca's mother always fixes her peanut butter and jelly sandwiches.

5. Andy's mother had sent tuna.

6. Andy was seen entering the classroom at the first recess.

7. Andy, Carol and Bianca all like cookies and all three had their lunches in brown paper bags.

8. Carol was the first one to be excused to get her lunch.

9. Andy is allergic to oranges.

10. Bianca keeps her lunch in her desk.

11. Andy and Carol keep their lunches on the shelf at the back of the room.

12. Andy's lunch sack had a chicken sandwich, an orange, and oatmeal cookies.

13. Bianca was crying and wanted her lunch back, which she thought should include a peanut butter and jelly sandwich and cookies.

14. Carol's mother only sends oatmeal cookies.

15. Bianca had seen her mother pack chocolate chip cookies in her lunch.

16. Today's date is April 1.

Solution _____

_____

Name_____

In each set of words the same letter has been replaced by a ☐ to form a stairway. On the line following each set write what the ☐ stands for. Remember the letter you pick to replace the ☐ must form a real word with each member of the set.

Example ☐eal
i☐ea
fa☐e
hee☐
☐ stands for d

1. ☐orn
a☐he
mi☐e
voi☐e
☐ stands for ____

2. ☐end
e☐ber
sa☐e
cla☐
☐ stands for ____

3. sel☐
gi☐t
a☐ter
☐ood
☐ stands for ____

4. gir☐
be☐t
b☐ue
☐ate
☐ stands for ____

5. ☐ite
s☐in
ra☐e
lar☐
☐ stands for ____

6. ☐ind
a☐ber
ga☐e
ter☐
☐ stands for ____

7. ☐ash
o☐it
ho☐e
ite☐
☐ stands for ____

8. ☐uff
s☐ade
co☐e
wee☐
☐ stands for ____

9. mai☐
ce☐t
s☐ag
☐eat
☐ stand for ____

10. bel☐
mo☐e
s☐am
☐and
☐ stand for ____

11. ☐ight
k☐it
se☐d
cor☐
☐ stands for ____

12. ☐ile
a☐ble
hy☐n
dee☐
☐stands for ____

44

Name_____

In each set of words the same letter has been replaced by a □ to form a stairway. On the line following each set write what the □ stands for. Remember the letter you pick to replace the □ must form a real word with each member of the set.

Example □hat
          a□om
          ac□or
          las□
          □ stands for t

1. □ice
   s□ap
   so□g
   loo□
   □ stands for _____

2. □art
   s□ark
   ho□e
   sou□
   □ stands for _____

3. see□
   mi□e
   i□age
   □ust
   □ stands for _____

4. bar□
   si□g
   s□ow
   □ick
   □ stands for _____

5. □ose
   f□et
   co□n
   dea□
   □ stands for _____

6. □ick
   i□n't
   va□e
   iri□
   □ stands for _____

7. □ane
   e□ery
   lo□e
   ali□e
   □ stands for _____

8. □ipe
   c□ew
   co□e
   tea□
   □ stands for _____

9. jes□
   bi□e
   i□em
   □erm
   □ stands for _____

10. chi□
    ta□e
    s□are
    □urr
    □ stands for _____

11. □ent
    o□ls
    la□n
    sho□
    □ stands for _____

12. □ide
    i□sue
    ca□t
    thu□
    □ stands for _____

Name _____

In each set of words the same letter has been replaced by a ☐ to form a stairway. On the line following each set write what the ☐ stands for. Remember the letter you pick to replace the ☐ must form a real word with each member of the set.

Example ☐amp
a☐es
di☐e
zin☐
☐ stands for c

1. ☐ary
e☐er
co☐e
hal☐e
☐ stands for ____

2. ☐our
t☐pe
ge☐ser
hol☐
☐ stands for ____

3. wes☐
ca☐s
i☐ch
☐ide
☐ stands for ____

4. ble☐
la☐s
o☐es
☐eek
☐ stands for ____

5. ☐ump
e☐it
hi☐e
cla☐
☐ stands for ____

6. ☐mit
c☐al
kn☐t
int☐
☐ stands for ____

7. ☐ook
s☐ob
te☐t
moo☐
☐ stands for ____

8. ☐ike
s☐ace
ro☐e
shi☐
☐ stands for ____

9. toa☐
od☐s
a☐ore
☐rum
☐ stands for ____

10. see☐
mo☐s
s☐ider
☐lay
☐ stands for ____

11. ☐ead
t☐ot
ca☐e
yea☐
☐ stands for ____

12. ☐eck
e☐ge
si☐e
loa☐
☐ stands for ____

Name _____

The object of these puzzles is to transform the word on the top line into the
word on the bottom line by changing only one letter at a time. To solve the
puzzles you must follow these rules:

1. Change only one of the four letters in each move.
2. Each new transformation must be a real word.
3. Change each letter only once.
4. Use only four turns to reach the goal word.

Example   stop
              shop
              ship
              chip
              chin

Since these puzzles are much more difficult than they appear, working them on
scrap paper first is recommended.

1. when	2. lock	3. free	4. moss	5. week
_____	_____	_____	_____	_____
_____	_____	_____	_____	_____
_____	_____	_____	_____	_____
team	rate	than	runt	moat

6. time	7. band	8. yarn	9. east	10. clay
_____	_____	_____	_____	_____
_____	_____	_____	_____	_____
_____	_____	_____	_____	_____
sand	leaf	wood	cove	stir

Name_____

The same word is missing in all four sentences in each set. Read each sentence carefully to discover the missing word. Remember the missing word must fit into each sentence in the set, and the sentences must make sense.

Set 1

No matter how _____ Jill tried, she could never keep up with her sisters.

We need a _____ , smooth surface for this experiment.

The puzzle was so _____ that only Tony and Tara finished it.

Kate's family had a _____ time while her father was out of work.

Set 2

Let's _____ up and get on the bus.

The fisherman cast his _____ into the river.

Clint hit a _____ drive to first base.

Mrs. Stevens sang as she hung the clothes on the _____ .

Set 3

I always use this _____ to take makeup off at night.

The dairy separates the _____ from the milk.

_____ the butter, sugar, and eggs before adding the dry ingredients.

The soup du jour is _____ of broccoli.

Set 4

The pony's _____ was long and shaggy.

Please sew this button on my wool _____ .

There was a fresh _____ of paint on the fence.

Dip the apple in the warm carmel to _____ it evenly.

Set 5

Will you make a list of the things that most _____ you?

The bank pays _____ on savings accounts.

We stopped on our trip at many points of _____ .

She owns a one-third _____ in the business.

Set 6

The aspirin offered immediate _____ for my headache.

The _____ pitcher came in during the fifth inning.

The contour was clearly illustrated on the _____ map.

Our community sent _____ to the disaster victims.

Name_____

You just found a message in a bottle that has washed up on the seashore. When you take the message out of the bottle, you find that it has been written in code. See if you can decipher the code and read the message.

Message

5 c2n j8st 5m2g5n4 th4 s8rpr5s4 s9m49n4 w5ll 4xp4r54nc4 wh4n th47 9p4n th5s b9ttl4 2nd d5sc9v4r th2t th4 m4ss2g4 5s w5tt4n 5n 2 sp4c52l c9d4. W4ll 5 th5nk th4 p4rs9n w5ll b4 v4r7 c8r598s 2nd w5ll w2nt t9 br42k th4 c9d4 2nd r42d th4 m4ss2g4. 2m 5 c9rr4ct? D9 798 2ls9 w9nd4r wh2t k5nd 9f p4rs9n w98ld d9 s8ch 2 cr2z7 th5ng? T9 f5nd th4 2nsw4r t9 th4 l2st q84st59n, br42k th4 c9d4 2nd wr5t4 t9 m4. M7 2ddr4ss 5s D2m9n Wr5t4, tw9 tw9 s5x H2v4rf9rd Pl2c4, J4ff4rs9n, M9. 5 w5ll l99k f9rw2rd t9 h42r5ng fr9m 2 c8r598s s9m49n4 s9m4t5m4.

Code

2 = _____
4 = _____
5 = _____
7 = _____
8 = _____
9 = _____

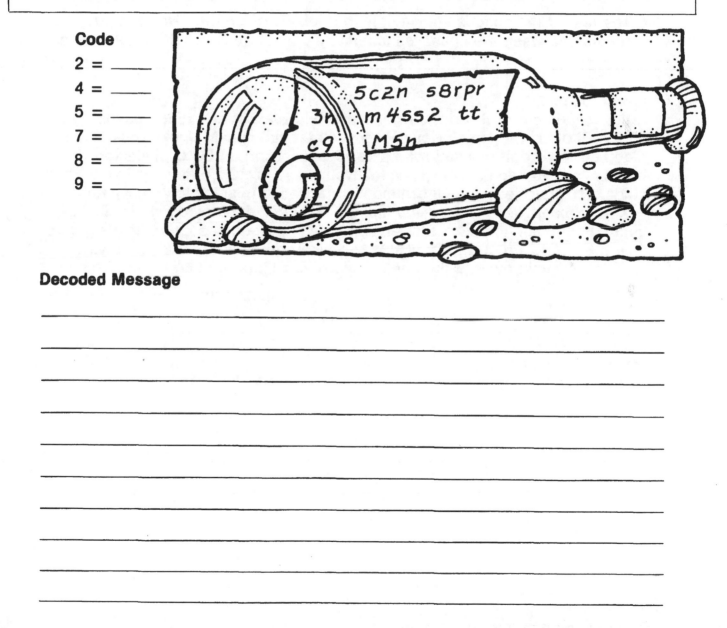

Decoded Message

_____

_____

_____

_____

_____

_____

_____

_____

_____

Name_____

Jennifer and Robby decided to write to one another in code. Before they sent their first message, they made up a code. Using the following clues, see if you can break the code and decipher the following message.

Clues

1. Vowels in our standard alphabet are represented in code by the vowel that follows them. And u is represented by a.

2. All the consonants in the alphabet that precede a vowel are represented in code as the consonant that immediately follows that vowel. For example, d is represented in code as f.

3. All the consonants that follow a vowel are coded as the consonant that immediately follows them. For example, f is coded as g.

4. The rest of the code is known only to Robby and Jennifer. However, by reading between the lines, you should be able to decipher the whole message.

Message

Fied Kippogid,

Jo. O xadi ipkuzif liivopy zua vjox xallid bjip zua woxovif zuad huaxopx, vji lludzx. Bi dierrz jef gap ev vjev eahvoup, vji fez zua cuayjv vjev epvosai cavvid hjadp epf ov vadpif uav vu jewi e judpiv'x pixv opxofi ug ov. O piwid xeb vji hdubf xvedv vu dap gexvid vjep vji eahvoupiid vermx. Og bi jefp'v ciip dappopy xu gexv bi buarf jewi xiip vji eahvoupiid epf Qedxup Saolcz fowi op vji hub qupf.

Xhjuur ox op xixxoup pub—pu ludi qohpohx epf xbollopy op vji dowid; kaxv budm, budm, epf julibudm. Ehvaerrz vjox zied ox xjeqopy aq vu ci ruvx ug gap. O jewi Ld. Xolqxup gud juliduul. Ji'x Iz cexicerr huehj epf dierrz e pohi yaz.

O'wi yuv vu yu pub epf jirq Fef jear ciepx vu vji lorr. Juqi O'wi yuv vji hufi doyjv.

Zuad xallid gdoipf,
Duccz

Solution

a b c d e f g h i j k l m n o p q r s t u v w x y z

_____

_____

_____

_____

Continue on another piece of paper.

Name _____

Inferences are "educated guesses." They are conclusions that are drawn from known information, but the conclusions are only partially supported by the information. Inferences take you from the known to the unknown. Inferencing involves reading between the lines, judging, and surmising. Some inferences are reasonable and some are not.

Example
Bobbi calls her dog in for dinner each night at 5:00 p.m. Each night he comes in wagging his tail as soon as he is called. It doesn't matter if she calls him Buster, Custer, Mister, Sister, or George. He always comes. Bobbi thinks that her dog must be trained to get his dinner each night at 5:00 and will come no matter what she says. Or he likes to be called different names just like she likes to be called Bobbi sometimes and Roberta sometimes.
The first inference is a correct one. The second inference is not a reasonable one.

Read the following statements and decide if the inferences are reasonable from the information that is given. In each case choose the most reasonable or logical explanation. Write "yes" if the inference is sound and "no" if it is not. Be ready to defend your answers.

1. Joan buys a new pair of shoes.
    a. Her old shoes are worn out. _____
    b. She needs a new pair of shoes to match her new dress. _____
    c. She found a pair of shoes she likes at a price she is willing to pay. _____

2. Betty doesn't eat her broccoli.
    a. Betty doesn't like green vegetables. _____
    b. Betty doesn't like broccoli. _____
    c. Betty isn't hungry. _____

3. Jason doesn't speak to his best friend, Robert, when he passes him in the hall.
    a. Jason did not see Robert. _____
    b. Jason is mad at Robert. _____
    c. Jason never speaks to anyone. _____

4. People who go to the Robust Gym always look thin and healthy.
    a. All the healthy, thin people go to the Robust gym. _____
    b. Going to the gym makes you thin and healthy. _____
    c. All the unhealthy people are at home in front of the television. _____

5. Byron got caught cheating on his spelling test.
    a. He didn't know how to spell the words on his own. _____
    b. The teacher doesn't like him. _____
    c. He will probably grow up and cheat on his income taxes. _____

Name _____

One area of logic looks at whether information given, statements made and questions asked about a situation are relevant. That is, do they have something to do with the matter at hand or are they related to the point being made?

Example
Bill cannot find his wallet and asks his brother if he has seen it. His brother replies, "Do you think I took it? I get blamed for everything. Even at school Mrs. Smith blames me when our row is the last one to get ready. No, I haven't seen your wallet."

Only one statement, the last one, is relevant to Bill's question.

Read these situations and decide which statements or questions are relevant. Put R by the relevant statements and NR by the statements that are not relevant.

1. Miss Jones asks Ralph why he does not have his math homework completed. He responds:
   _____ He did not understand how to do the math and neither did his parents.
   _____ Joyce didn't do her spelling homework last night either.
   _____ Math is his favorite subject.
   _____ His family was away from home until late last night.
   _____ He really likes the dress she's wearing today.

2. Jed is trying to convince his mother that she should take him to school rather than making him ride his bike. His arguments are:
   _____ His bike is ugly.
   _____ It's raining and he'll get wet.
   _____ He's late and will be late to school if he rides.
   _____ She's such a nice mother.
   _____ She bakes wonderful chocolate chip cookies.

3. Robin thinks she would like to try out for the swim team and is making a list of all the reasons why she should. Her reasons are:
   _____ She enjoys swimming.
   _____ Her friend, Becky, is on the basketball team.
   _____ She's a good swimmer.
   _____ She's also good at ballet.
   _____ Swimming is good exercise.

4. Jimmy is writing an article on the baseball team for the school paper. The title of the article is "Panthers Slide into First Place." Which facts should he use?
   _____ The uniforms are red and white.
   _____ The team won the last game 3-0.
   _____ The team has won 10 out of 12 games.
   _____ Many of the players on the team are nice.
   _____ Matt, the pitcher, has pitched six no-hit games.

Name _____

When two incidents happen at the same time or close to the same time, they are sometimes related in such a way that one thing causes the other. For instance, hitting the ball with the bat makes it fly through the air.

cause: hitting the ball
effect: ball flies through air

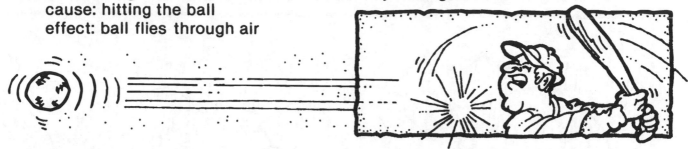

Sometimes people make errors in reasoning by saying that one thing causes another when they are not related, but merely happen at the same time or within a short time frame.

Read the following statements and match the cause with the effect.

Cause	Effect
1. ____ If you're late for school	a. it will break.
2. ____ If you deprive a plant of water and light	b. it will rust.
3. ____ If you drop an egg on the floor	c. it will die.
4. ____ If you leave your bike out in the rain	d. you'll make up the time after school.

Read the following statements and decide If there is a logical cause-effect relationship between the happenings. Write "yes" or "no" on the line.

5. _____ Tanya notices that whenever she washes her jeans they are tight. She reasons that washing the jeans must shrink them.

6. _____ Tom crosses his fingers while walking to the plate because that will make him hit the ball farther.

7. _____ Norene notices that there is a high tide whenever there is a full moon. She decides that the high tide must cause the moon to be full.

8. _____ Whenever it rains the hills turn green. Tom thinks that the rain must cause the hills to change color.

9. _____ Bertha notices that whenever she forgets her lunch and her mother has to bring it to her, her mother is in a grouchy mood. She thinks that maybe her forgetfulness causes her mother's bad mood.

10. _____ Whenever there are clouds in the sky it rains. Bobby thinks there cannot be rain without clouds.

11. _____ As a result of an extensive campaign to vaccinate children, there has been a decrease in the numbers of children who get measles.

12. _____ Mr. Jones finds himself in a traffic jam at 5:00 p.m. each day. He notices that the other drivers seem unhappy. He thinks that getting off work must make them unhappy.

13. _____ Each fall the leaves of some trees turn colors and then drop to the ground. The trees that do not change color, do not drop their leaves. Therefore, the color change must cause the trees to drop their leaves.

Name _____

In logic, we use special notation to show logic sentences or phrases. We use capital letters to stand for events. We can use a single letter or double letters. We also can use → to mean "if-then" or "it follows that" or "implies."

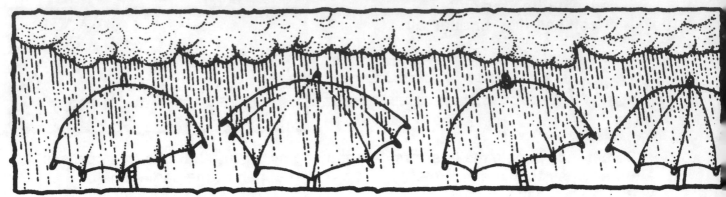

Example 1
R stands for "it rains"
U stands for "I'll bring my umbrella"
So we can say "If it rains, then I'll bring my umbrella."
          If R, then U
          R → U

Example 2
CB = car is broken
WW = we'll walk
Then we can say "If the car is broken, then we will walk."
          If CB, then WW
          CB → WW

Example 3
"If John comes, then Gary will be happy" could be written JC → GH.

Match these conditional statements with their notations.

1. ____ If Jane comes, Bob will come too.   a. CB → W

2. ____ If you sing, then the dog will bark.   b. S → T

3. ____ If you speed, you'll get a ticket.   c. BO → PF

4. ____ If the car is broken, we'll walk.   d. J → B

5. ____ If the book is over-due, I'll pay the fine.   e. YS → DB

6. ____ If you eat peas, then you can have dessert.   f. P → D

54

Name _____

As you remember, you can use capital letters to stand for single thoughts in logic. You can also use this notation to show statements that include the words "and" or "or."

"If you clean your room and do the dishes, then I'll help" would be

written (CR and DD) → IH.

"If you walk or you ride, then I'll come" would be written (YW or YR) → IC.

Write the following statements in logical notation using the symbols that are given.

1. If you eat that, then you'll get sick. (E,S) _____

2. If I were you, I would go. (IY, IG) _____

3. If we're given a choice, then I'll chose fudge. (GC, CF) _____

4. If the rose is red, then I'll pick it. (RR, IP) _____

5. If Josh comes, then there will be three. (T, JC). _____

6. If it rains or snows, then we'll go to the show. (R, S, GS). _____

7. If Janet sneezes, then everyone will laugh or yawn. (JS, EL, EY). _____

8. If I study and get rest, then I'll do good on the test. (S,R,G) _____

9. If Mark comes and Jeff stays, we'll have a team. (JS, WT, MC). _____

Write if-then statements of your own and show each statement in logical notation.

10. _____

_____

11. _____

_____

Name _____

The negation of a statement is a statement that has a different truth value. That is, if a statement is true, it's negation would be false.

Example
Statement: "Jill is smart."
Negation: "Jill is not smart."
             "Jill is dumb" is not the negation.

We note the negation of a statement with the symbol ~ in front of a capital letter that indicates the event. So the negation of A is ~A.
~A means not A or A is false.

Example
B stands for "The dog is barking."
~B stands for "The dog is not barking" or "It is false that the dog is barking."

Write the negation of each of these statements and show the symbol for the negation.

statement	negation	symbol
1. The car is red . (CR)		
2. Jack is tall . (JT)		
3. The paper is torn . (PT)		
4. We won the race . (W)		
5. It's raining . (R)		

Name _____

Fill in the chart so each line has a statement, a symbol for the statement, a negation, and a symbol for the negation.

statement	symbol	negated statement	negated symbol
1. Bob rides his bike to school.	RB		
2. Jamie is a Boy Scout.	JS		
3. It is cold.			~C
4. Justin plays piano.	JP		
5. I'll wash dishes.			
6. Bob can come.			
7. It's your turn.			
8.		John is not sick	
9.		It is false that Karen knew.	
10.		The cat will not come in.	~CC
11.		It is not hot.	~H
12. It costs a lot.			
13. Your room is messy.			

Name _____

Sometimes we find the words "and" or "or" in statements in logic. These are statements like:

    John likes peppermint and Kate likes chocolate. (JP and KC)
    John likes peppermint or Kate likes chocolate. (JP or KC)

To negate an "and" statement, negate each part and change the "and" to "or."
    ~(JP and KC) = ~JP or ~KC
John doesn't like peppermint or Kate doesn't like chocolate.

To negate an "or" statement, negate each part and change the "or" to "and."
    ~(JP or KC) = ~JP and ~KC
John doesn't like peppermint and Kate doesn't like chocolate.

Example
(CP and DT) = The cow is purple and the dog talks.

~(CP and DT) = (~CP or ~DT) = The cow is not purple or the dog does not talk.

~(CP or DT) = (~CP and ~DT) = The cow is not purple and the dog does not talk.

Fill in the chart with the negation and the symbol for the negation for each statement.

statement	symbol	negation	symbol
1. I will go and I'll take you. (G and T)			
2. Dick will go and Bill will stay. (DG and BS)			
3. Dogs bark and chickens cackle. (DB and CC)			
4. Cats have fur or fish have scales. (CF or FS)			
5. You'll eat it all or you'll get hungry. (YE or YH)			
6. Bill will make cookies or Joy will make pie. (BC or JP)			
7. He has a beard and she has blond hair. (HB and SB)			

Name _____

Match the following statements with their logical notation.

1. If the dog barks, then the cat will howl.
2. If John works, he'll get rich.
3. If this flies, I'll eat my hat.
4. If Judy enters, she'll win.
5. If my sandwich has butter or my apple is mushy, then I'll throw my lunch away.
6. If June comes and Adam doesn't, then it won't be fun.
7. If the pop pops and the fizzle fizzles, then the gong won't gong.
8. Madge came and Joe left.

a. F → EH
b. E → W
c. J and ∼A → ∼F
d. DB → CH
e. P and F → ∼G
f. B or M → T
g. W → R
h. MC and JL

Write the negation of each statement and the symbol for the negation.

symbol	statement	negated symbol	negation
9. R	A rose is red.		
10. B	Burns hurt.		
11. T	That's tough.		
12. A and J	Adam and Juan both came.		
13. BD and MC	Bring pop and make a cake.		
14. RF and ∼LP	Red is my favorite color and I don't like purple		
15. C and ∼J	Jamil likes fish and Joe does not.		
16. TN	Ted is my neighbor.		
17. BB	The button broke.		

Name _____

Two statements are said to be equivalent if one statement can replace the other. Equivalent statements have the same truth values. The symbol for equivalence is ≡. Every statement is equivalent to itself and its double negation.

So if A = All ants have six legs.
~A = All ants don't have six legs.
~~A = It is false that all ants don't have six legs.
So A ≡ ~~A

Match each statement with an equivalent statement.

1. ~~B   a. ~B
2. A   b. ~~BM
3. BM   c. D and F
4. ~~BF   d. B
5. ~~(A and B) e. BF
6. ~(~D or ~F) f. A and B
7. ~(~~B)   g. ~~A

For each statement, write an equivalent statement. To help you, the logical symbols for each statement are given.

8. Beatrice has the measles. (BM)

_____

9. It is false that Joe can't come. (~~JC)

_____

10. Birds can fly. (BF)

_____

11. Joe is pitcher and Carrie is catcher. (JP and CC)

_____

12. Cyndi works hard. (CW)

_____

13. Cyndi works hard and Lynda plays. (CW and LP)

_____

14. Cyndi does not work hard. (~CW)

_____

Name _____

Use the symbols by each statement to show the statement in logical notation.

1. The milk is sour and the food is cold. (MS, FC) _____

2. You are in school or you are at work. (YS, YW) _____

3. The wagon is red and the car is not blue. (WR, CB) _____

4. It is false that Jim is tall. (JT) _____

5. I don't like pickles and Mike doesn't like nuts. (IP, MN) _____

6. Lisa isn't blond or Maura had red hair. (LB, MR) _____

7. That joke is not funny. (JF) _____

8. It is false that the joke is not funny. (JF) _____

Remember that two statements are equivalent if they can replace each other and have the same truth value. A statement is equivalent to itself and its double negation.

Write each statement one other way (an equivalent statement) and write the symbol for the equivalent statement.

9. The robin is in her nest. _____

10. It is false that Joy is not smart. _____

11. Troy has red hair. _____

12. It is false that I'm going and Joyce is staying. _____

13. Joe doesn't like peanuts or Carrie doesn't like walnuts. _____

Answers

Lesson 1
1. yes	5. yes	9. no
2. no	6. yes	10. no
3. no	7. no	11. yes
4. no	8. yes	12. yes

A hertog is a figure having at least two curved parts.

Lesson 2
1. yes	5. no	9. no
2. yes	6. yes	10. no
3. yes	7. yes	11. no
4. no	8. yes	12. yes

A jayzel is any closed figure with a dot inside.

Lesson 3
1. no	5. no	9. yes
2. yes	6. yes	10. yes
3. yes	7. yes	11. yes
4. no	8. no	12. yes

A notaddel is any closed figure with an even number of protrusions.

Lesson 4
1. yes	5. no	9. yes
2. yes	6. yes	10. no
3. no	7. no	11. yes
4. yes	8. no	12. no

A cinqueen is any figure that contains five straight lines.

Lesson 5
1. things that are white
2. things with double letters
3. things with holes
4. things that begin with c
5. things with two syllables
6. things that are large

Lesson 6
1. c	4. b
2. c	5. c
3. c	6. a

Lesson 7
1. b	4. a
2. b	5. a
3. a	6. c

Lesson 8
1. d	5. d	9. d
2. c	6. a	10. c
3. b	7. d	11. c
4. c	8. c	12. d

Lesson 9
1. a	5. c	9. a
2. d	6. d	10. c
3. c	7. b	11. c
4. b	8. d	12. b

Lesson 10
1. d	5. b	9. d
2. a	6. d	10. a
3. c	7. d	11. b
4. d	8. a	12. b

Lesson 11
1. b	5. c	9. b
2. b	6. c	10. c
3. d	7. d	11. d
4. c	8. d	12. b

Lesson 12
1. d	5. c	9. d
2. c	6. a	10. b
3. c	7. d	11. d
4. b	8. a	12. a

Lesson 13
1. c	5. d	9. d
2. b	6. c	10. c
3. c	7. c	11. c
4. d	8. b	12. a

Lesson 14
1. b	5. b	9. a
2. c	6. c	10. b
3. c	7. c	11. b
4. c	8. c	12. b

Lesson 15
1. d	5. c	9. b
2. b	6. d	10. d
3. b	7. a	11. b
4. a	8. c	12. a

Lesson 16
1. a	5. b	9. c
2. c	6. b	10. d
3. b	7. a	11. d
4. d	8. b	12. c

Lesson 17
1. a	5. d	9. d
2. b	6. b	10. c
3. c	7. c	11. c
4. b	8. a	12. b

Lesson 18
2, 7, 9, 1, 3, 4, 12, 6, 10, 13, 5, 8, 11

Lesson 19
3, 5, 8, 12, 1, 7, 9, 10, 2, 6, 11, 4

Lesson 20
4, 7, 1, 6, 2, 8, 3, 9, 5

Lesson 21
1. valid
2. valid
3. invalid
4. invalid
5. valid

Lesson 22
1. invalid
2. invalid
3. invalid
4. valid
5. valid
6. invalid
7. invalid
8. invalid
9. invalid
10. invalid
11. valid
12. valid
13. invalid
14. invalid

Lesson 23
1. valid
2. invalid
3. Invalid
4. valid
5. invalid
6. invalid
7. invalid
8. invalid
9. valid
10. invalid
11. valid
12. invalid
13. invalid

Lesson 24
1. valid
2. invalid
3. invalid
4. valid
5. invalid
6. invalid
7. valid
8. valid
9. invalid
10. valid
11. invalid
12. invalid
13. valid
14. invalid

Lesson 25
1. all whales give live birth.
2. no lizards are warm-blooded.
3. Mickey has a tail.
4. Donald cannot bark.
5. no crooks are happy.
6. George likes snow.
7. all frogs hatched from eggs.
8. spiders have eight legs.
9. ice contains oxygen.
10. all gumps are slimy.
11. no lions are herbivores.
12. no fleebles are free.
13. 276,454 is divisible by two.

Lesson 26
1. Everest is not small.
2. Freckles is funny.
3. boys are adorable.
4. no cats are prickly.
5. cows are part of the food chain.
6. insects frighten me.
7. all rabbits eat plants.
8. a lawn mower makes work easier.
9-10. answers will vary.

Lesson 27
answers left to right:
Mets, Phillies, Cubs, Cardinals, Pirates, Expos

Lesson 28
answers left to right:
Old Yeller, red
Robinson Crusoe, blue
Kidnapped, black
Gulliver's Travels, brown
Savage Sam, brown
Tom Sawyer, brown

Lesson 29
clockwise from empty chair:
Ken - chicken nuggets
Maggie - taco salad
Bob - quarter-pound cheeseburger
Drew - fish sandwich
Jolie - roast beef sandwich

Lesson 30
Brian, 9, blueberry
Andrew, 10½, cherry
Mike, 10, grape
Robby, 11, orange

Lesson 31
Brendan Ming, head guard, 18
Catherine Cowell, diving coach, 15
Donald Pearlstein, assistant manager, 18
Suzanne Graham, swim team coach, 17
Paul Becker, swimming lessons, 16

Lesson 32
Becky Brown, worms, most
Michelle Cardwell, worms, smallest
Jimmy McDonnell, crickets, biggest
Curt Fisher, minnows, first

Lesson 33
Ken Dominguez, group 4, Cat Country
Kimberly McCann, group 3, Primate House
Brian Roberts, group 2, Bear Pits
Jennifer Bouler, group 1, Reptile House

Lesson 34
Ashley, 9 months, 9:00
Robby, 2½ years, 6:00
Sean, 3 months, 7:00
Casey, 5, 8:00
Dana, 1 year, 6:30

Lesson 35
Jonathan Baxter, soccer net, $1.00
Monica Staehle, lighted mirror, $2.50
Tom Mano, clock, $.50
Matthew Kincaid, skateboard, $2.75

Lesson 36
Bob Anastasi, Mon.-Wed.-Fri., 9th
Candy Reardon, Wed.-Fri., 9th
David Rodriguez, Tues.-Thurs.- Sat., 10th
Elvina Gerber, Fri.- Sat., 11th

Lesson 37

Mikie tracked in mud when he came in to get cookies for the other children.

Lesson 38

Andy switched lunches with Bianca at recess, as an April Fool's joke. Carol took Andy's lunch sack by mistake.

Lesson 39

1. c	5. k	9. n
2. m	6. m	10. l
3. f	7. m	11. n
4. l	8. p	12. m

Lesson 40

1. n	5. r	9. t
2. p	6. s	10. p
3. m	7. v	11. w
4. n	8. r	12. s

Lesson 41

1. v	5. d	9. d
2. y	6. o	10. p
3. t	7. n	11. r
4. w	8. p	12. d

Lesson 42

1. when	2. lock	3. free	4. moss	5. week
then	lack	tree	most	meek
them	rack	thee	must	meet
teem	race	then	rust	meat
team	rate	than	runt	moat

6. time	7. band	8. yarn	9. east	10. clay
tame	land	yard	cast	slay
same	lend	ward	case	stay
sane	lead	word	cave	star
sand	leaf	wood	cove	stir

Lesson 43

1. hard	5. interest
2. line	6. relief
3. cream	
4. coat	

Lesson 44

2 = a	5 = i	8 = u
4 = e	7 = y	9 = o

I can just imagine the surprise someone will experience when they open this bottle and discover that the message is written in a special code. Well I think the person will be very curious and will want to break the code and read the message. Am I correct? Do you also wonder what kind of a person would do such a crazy thing? To find the answer to the last question, break the code and write to me. My address is Damon Write, two two six Haverford Place, Jefferson, MO. I will look forward to hearing from a curious someone sometime.

Lesson 45

Dear Jennifer,

Hi. I sure enjoyed meeting you this summer when you visited your cousins, the Emorys. We really had fun at that auction, the day you bought that antique butter churn and it turned out to have a hornet's nest inside of it. I never saw the crowd start to run faster than the auctioneer talks. If we hadn't been running so fast we would have seen the auctioneer and Parson Quimby dive in the cow pond.

School is in session now—no more picnics and swimming in the river; just work, work, and homework. Actually this year is shaping up to be lots of fun. I have Mr Simpson for homeroom. He's my baseball coach and really a nice guy.

I've got to go now and help Dad haul beans to the mill. Hope I've got the code right.

Your summer friend,
Robby

Lesson 46

Answers may vary depending on the reasoning involved. Answers should be discussed and students should be able to defend any answers they give. The most typical reasoning would yield the following answers:

1. a. no	4. a. no
b. no	b. yes
c. yes	c. no
2. a. no	
b. yes	
c. maybe, it doesn't say if that is all Betty has on her plate.	
3. a. yes	5. a. yes
b. no	b. no
c. no	c. no

Lesson 47

1. R, NR, NR, R, NR
2. NR, R, R, NR, NR
3. R, NR, R, NR, R
4. NR, R, R, NR, R

Lesson 48

1. d	5. yes	9. yes
2. c	6. no	10. yes
3. a	7. no	11. yes
4. b	8. yes	12. no
		13. no

Lesson 49

1. d
2. e
3. b
4. a
5. c
6. f

Lesson 50
1. E → S
2. IY → IG
3. GC → CF
4. RR → IP
5. JC → T
6. (R or S) → GS
7. JS → (EL or EY)
8. (S and R) → G
9. (MC and JS) → WT
10-11. answers will vary

Lesson 51
1. The car is not red.   ~CR
2. Jack is not tall.   ~JT
3. The paper is not torn. ~PT
4. We didn't win the race. ~W
5. It's not raining.   ~R

Lesson 52
Where students are allowed to make up their own symbols, they may be different from those given below.
1. Bob does not ride his bike to school. ~RB
2. Jamie is not a Boy Scout. ~JS
3. C, It is not cold.
4. Justin does not play the piano. ~JP
5. WD, I won't wash dishes. ~WD
6. BC, Bob can't come. ~BC
7. YT, It's not your turn. ~YT
8. John is sick, JS, ~JS
9. Karen knew. KK, ~KK
10. The cat will come in. CC
11. It is hot. H
12. CL, It does not cost a lot. ~CL
13. RM, Your room is not messy. ~RM

Lesson 53
1. I will not go or I won't take you. (~G or ~T)
2. Dick will not go or Bill will not stay. (~DG or ~BS)
3. Dogs don't bark or chickens don't cackle. (~DB or ~CC)
4. Cats don't have fur and fish don't have scales. (~CF and ~FS)
5. You won't eat it all and you won't get hungry. (~YE and ~YH)
6. Bill won't make cookies and Joy won't make pie. (~BC and ~JP)
7. He doesn't have a beard or she doesn't have blond hair. (~HB or ~SB)

Lesson 54
1. d   5. f
2. g   6. c
3. a   7. e
4. b   8. h

9. ~R, A rose is not red.
10. ~B, Burns don't hurt.
11. ~T, That's not tough.
12. ~A or ~J, Adam didn't come or Juan didn't come.
13. ~BD or ~MC, Don't bring pop or don't make a cake.
14. ~RF or LP, Red is not my favorite color or I like purple.
15. ~C or J, Jamil doesn't like fish or Joe does.
16. ~TN, Ted is not my neighbor.
17. ~BB, The button didn't break.

Lesson 55
1. d
2. g
3. b
4. e
5. f
6. c
7. a
8. It is false that Beatrice doesn't have the measles.
9. Joe can come.
10. It is false that birds can't fly.
11. It is false that Joe is not the pitcher or Carrie is not the catcher.
12. It is false that Cyndi doesn't work hard.
13. It is false the Cyndi doesn't work hard or Lynda doesn't play.
14. It is false that Cyndi works hard.

Lesson 56
1. MS and FC
2. YS or YW
3. WR and ~CB
4. ~JT
5. ~IP and ~MN
6. ~BB or MR
7. ~JF
8. ~~JF
9. It is false that the robin is not in her nest. ~~~RN
10. Joy is smart. JS
11. It is false that Troy doesn't have red hair. ~~~TR
12. I am not going or Joyce is not staying ~IG or ~JS
13. It is false that Joe likes peanuts and Carrie likes walnuts. ~(JP and CW)

Common Core State Standards Alignment Sheet
Logic Liftoff

Lesson	Common Core State Standards
Relationships (Lessons 1-5)	ELA-Literacy: L.4.5, L.5.5 &, L.6.5 Demonstrate understanding of figurative language, word relationships and nuances in word meanings.
Analogies (Lessons 6-14)	Math: 4.OA.C Generate and analyze patterns. 5.OA.B Analyze patterns and relationships. ELA-Literacy: L.4.5, L.5.5, & L.6.5 Demonstrate understanding of figurative language, word relationships and nuances in word meanings.
Sequences (Lessons 15-20)	Math: 4.OA.C Generate and analyze patterns. 5.OA.B Analyze patterns and relationships.
Syllogisms (Lessons 21-26)	ELA/Literacy: CCRA.R.8 Delineate and evaluate the argument and specific claims in a text, including the validity of the reasoning as well as the relevance and sufficiency of the evidence.
Deduction (Lessons 27-38)	ELA/Literacy: RI.4.1 Refer to details and examples in a text when explaining what the text says explicitly and when drawing inferences from the text.
Inferencing (Lessons 39-45)	ELA/Literacy: RI.4.1 Refer to details and examples in a text when explaining what the text says explicitly and when drawing inferences from the text. L.4.5, L.5.5 &, L.6.5 Demonstrate understanding of figurative language, word relationships, and nuances in word meanings.
Logical Reasoning (Lessons 46-48)	ELA/Literacy: RI.4.1 Refer to details and examples in a text when explaining what the text says explicitly and when drawing inferences from the text. RI.5.5 Compare and contrast the overall structure (e.g., chronology, comparison, cause/effect, problem/solution) of events, ideas, concepts, or information in two or more texts.
Logical Notation (Lessons 49-56)	RI.4.1 Refer to details and examples in a text when explaining what the text says explicitly and when drawing inferences from the text.

Printed in the United States
by Baker & Taylor Publisher Services